Somali Heritage

Celebrating Diversity in My Classroom

By Tamra B. Orr

21st Century
Junior Library

Published in the United States of America by
Cherry Lake Publishing
Ann Arbor, Michigan
www.cherrylakepublishing.com

Reading Adviser: Cecilia Minden, PhD, Literacy expert and children's author

Photo Credits: ©Homo Cosmicos/Shutterstock, cover; ©Stocktrek Images/Shutterstock, 4; ©Creative Photo Corner/Shutterstock, 6; ©FS Stock/Shutterstock, 8; ©Zurijeta/Shutterstock, 10; ©hayden carlyon/Shutterstock, 12; ©Sergey Fatin/Shutterstock, 14; ©Martinez de la Varga/Shutterstock, 16; ©Riccardo Mayer/Shutterstock, 18; ©Alex Kolokythas Photography/Shutterstock, 20

Library of Congress Cataloging-in-Publication Data has been filed and is available at catalog.loc.gov

Cherry Lake Publishing would like to acknowledge the work of the Partnership for 21st Century Skills. Please visit *www.p21.org* for more information.

Printed in the United States of America
Corporate Graphics

CONTENTS

Somalia is located in the Horn of Africa. It juts out into the Indian Ocean.

Surprising Somalia

Somalia is on the east coast of Africa. It is a bit smaller than Texas. Two sides are bordered by water. The other two are bordered by Djibouti, Ethiopia, and Kenya.

Somalia has a population of just over 11 million people. Many live in the capital city of Mogadishu. Most of Somalia is flat, with a few hills in the north.

In the past, thousands of Somalians fled their homeland. Many have come to the United States.

Unlike Arabic, the Somali language uses all the letters of the English alphabet except p, v, and z.

Barasho Wanaagsan!

Somalia has two official languages: Somali and Arabic. Somali is understood throughout the country. It is considered Somalia's primary language. People speak Arabic in northern and coastal towns. It is also the language used in most religious writings. "Pleased to meet you!" in Somali is *"Barasho wanaagsan!"* In Arabic, it is *"Salaam alaykum!"*

Before Somalia's independence in 1960, Italian was
the country's official language.

If you listen closely, however, you may also hear English. It is the most popular foreign language in Somalia. It is taught in many of the schools. A few other languages are spoken in rural parts of Somalia. For example, in the southern regions, some people speak Bravanese, Kibajuni, or Mushunguli.

Christians in Somalia practice in secret.
They risk being harassed by others.

Ramadan and Jinns

Almost all of the people in Somalia are Muslim, or followers of Islam. Like Muslims in other countries, Somalia's Muslims pray five times a day. Muslims also avoid drinking alcohol or eating pork. In Somalia, men are allowed to have as many as four wives at a time. Like other Muslim women, Somalian Muslim women wear **veils** and keep their bodies covered. Somalians observe Ramadan,

Jinns originated from the Quran, a religious text.
Rural women are more likely to encounter jinn.

a month-long period where no one eats or drinks between sunrise and sunset.

Some older people and people living far from cities hold ancient beliefs about the spirit world. They think *jinns*, or spirits, have the power to do good or evil things.

Sambusas are also called samosas. They are eaten throughout the Middle East, North Africa, Southeast Asia, and the region around India.

Sambusa and Sabaayad

Somalia does not have a national dish. But it does have a number of items that appear at almost every meal. Rice, bread, or spaghetti is commonly served. Somalians know how to add just the right seasonings to these ingredients to bring out their flavor! Rice is flavored with rich herbs and spices. Bread and noodles are usually dipped in a hot sauce called *shigni*. It is made of green chilies, tomatoes, coriander leaves, and

The world has around 14 million camels.
Somalia farms more than 7 million of them.

lemon juice. Somalia's flat bread is called *sabaayad*, and it is eaten at every meal. Flat bread made from corn, known as *muufo*, is a **staple** and usually topped with butter and honey. Sambusa is a triangle-shaped pastry filled with spicy meat or vegetables.

People living on farms and in the fields raise camels, goats, and cows. Families depend on the meat and milk from these animals.

Create!

Most Somalians do not use any utensils when they eat. Instead, they use their right hand. What would you serve at a meal with no utensils? Make a list of the most common "finger foods" and, with permission, create a meal. How would you include soup? What could you use for scooping food off your plate? Use your imagination!

Many people in Somalia lack clean drinking water.
Undrinkable water can cause illnesses like cholera.

Drought and Pirates

One of the biggest problems for Somalians is ongoing **drought** and **famine**. For several years, the country has not received enough rain. So growing food has become difficult. Livestock and crops have died. Many charity organizations have moved into Somalia to try and help. But life there is still very difficult.

Some Somalians, especially young men, have turned to a different way to survive. They have become pirates. Armed with dangerous

To keep pirates away, container ships began having armed guards. There is also an international fleet of ships to protect container ships.

weapons, these pirates attack tankers and **container ships**. They take **hostages** and cargo that they can exchange for money.

The lack of food and water, the poverty, and the rising crime levels are big problems. Like everyone else, Somalis want a safe place to live, raise their families, and have a future.

Look!

Camels are the country's most widely recognized symbol. Camels are used for traveling from one place to another. They can be bought and sold. They can be raised for meat and milk. Camels are also used to show someone's rank in society. The more camels you have, the richer you must be!

GLOSSARY

container ships (kuhn-TAYN-ur SHIPS) large boats designed to carry goods packaged in big metal boxes or barrels

drought (DROUT) a long period without rain; droughts can damage crops and dry out the soil

famine (FAM-in) a serious lack of food in an area

hostages (HAH-stij-iz) people held as prisoners by someone who is demanding something, such as money, before those people will be released

staple (STAY-puhl) a main product that is grown or made in a country or region

veils (VAYLZ) pieces of fabric worn by women as a covering for the head or face

Somalian Words

Barasho wanaagsan (buh-RAH-show wuh-NAG-sen) Pleased to meet you

muufo (MOO-foh) flat bread made from corn, a staple usually topped with butter and honey

sabaayad (suh-BAH-yahd) Somalian flat bread

sambusa (sam-BOO-suh) triangle-shaped pastry filled with spicy meat or vegetables

shigni (SHIG-nee) hot sauce

Arabic Words

jinns (JINZ) spirits that have the power to be good or evil

Salaam alaykum (suh-LAHM ah-LAY-kum) Pleased to meet you

FIND OUT MORE

BOOKS

Barghoorn, Linda. *A Refugee's Journey from Somalia.* New York: Crabtree Publishing Company, 2018.

Markovics, Adam. Somalia. New York: Bearport Publishing Company, 2018.

Owings, Lisa. *Somalia.* Minneapolis: Bellwether Media, 2015.

WEBSITES

Ducksters—Somalia
www.ducksters.com/geography/country.php?country=Somalia
Learn fast facts about Somalia's economy, history, and more.

Just Fun Facts—Interesting Facts About Somalia
www.justfunfacts.com/interesting-facts-about-somalia/
This link guides you through facts and photos of life in Somalia.

Multicultural Kid Blogs—10 Facts About Somalia
www.multiculturalkidblogs.com/2017/07/28/facts-somalia/
Discover even more about Somalia.

INDEX

ABOUT THE AUTHOR

Tamra Orr is the author of hundreds of books for readers of all ages. She graduated from Ball State University, but moved with her husband and four children to Oregon in 2001. She is a full-time author, and when she isn't researching and writing books, she writes letters to friends all over the world. Orr enjoys life in the big city of Portland and feels very lucky to be surrounded by so much diversity.